Swimmi...
Safely

by Sam Brelsfoard

PEARSON

Scott
Foresman

Editorial Offices: Glenview, Illinois • Parsippany, New Jersey • New York, New York
Sales Offices: Needham, Massachusetts • Duluth, Georgia • Glenview, Illinois
Coppell, Texas • Ontario, California • Mesa, Arizona

5 6 7 8 9 10 V0G1 14 13 12 11 10 09 08 07

CONTENTS

....

The Oceans' Currents

The ocean is an incredible and wild place. It can be a lot of fun to swim in, but it can also be dangerous. Have you ever been swimming in the ocean? If so, you have probably noticed that the ocean's water moves quite a bit.

Some beaches have large, powerful waves, while others have practically no waves at all. One thing that all oceans have in common, though, is that their water is always moving and circulating through currents.

A current is a section of water that moves continuously in one direction. There are many different kinds of currents, including deep water currents and rip currents. These currents can move very quickly and carry away things that may be caught in them.

This means that sometimes the water near the shore can be dangerous to swim in. Other times, the current is not as strong, and the water becomes safe for swimming. It is important to know how to recognize currents near the shore and what do to if you get caught in one. Let's discover how the oceans' currents work and how to swim safely in them.

The major oceans of the world are the Pacific Ocean, the Atlantic Ocean, the Indian Ocean, and the Arctic Ocean. Together, these oceans cover about 70 percent of Earth's surface. Water is constantly moving among these oceans through currents.

These currents exist both on and below the surface of the water. Surface currents travel along the top layer of the sea. They can be more than one hundred meters deep.

Deep water currents move below surface currents. They consist of saltier, colder water.

Oceanic water moves and circulates for a number of reasons and in many different ways. For example, solar heating causes water to expand, which sets it in motion.

Temperature and density also play a role in water movement. The colder and saltier the water is, the denser and heavier it gets. It sinks toward the bottom of the ocean. The warmer, less salty water rises toward the surface. This creates a constant up-and-down movement of water.

Wind and gravity also cause currents. Both of these forces push the ocean water along in different directions. So ocean water is constantly moving up, down, and in every other direction!

The oceans' fastest-moving currents are on the surface, where the water is lighter and less dense. Different types of currents have different names.

Four types of moving water are covered in this book. All of them pose a threat to swimmers. These are called lateral currents, rip currents, shorebreak, and backwash. Each one of these currents can be found at the shoreline. It is important that swimmers keep a sharp eye out for them before they venture into the water. Let's take a look at them, one at a time.

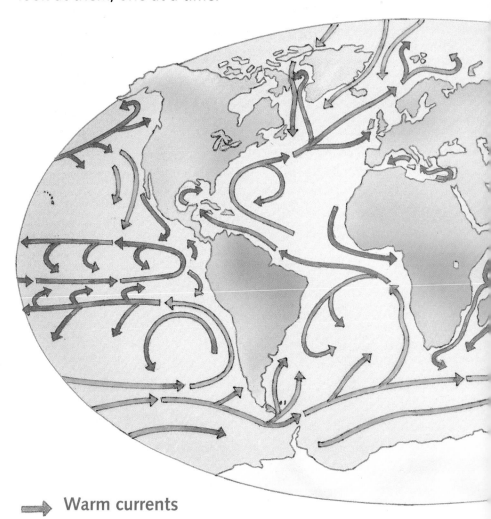

➡ Warm currents

Lateral Currents

Most waves break at an angle when they reach the shoreline. As they do this, they push water to the side. The water that is pushed aside creates a lateral current (also called a littoral, side, or longshore current) that moves water parallel to the shoreline.

These currents can be either fast- or slow-moving. The larger the waves, the stronger the lateral current. Most often they are slow-moving bodies of water that pose no real threat to a swimmer.

If, however, a lateral current combines with other currents, a potentially dangerous situation could arise.

A rip current, or a current that pulls water out to sea, forms when the lateral current hits an obstacle, such as a pier or sandbar, and forces water out to sea. Currents can be very hazardous to a swimmer if the swimmer doesn't know how to respond properly.

⇨ Cold currents

Rip Currents

Rip currents are created by the movement of water as it gathers at the shoreline, following the wake of a crashing wave. After a wave breaks, the water rushes back off the shore and into the ocean. This is when the rip current is formed. The strength of a rip current is generally relative to the size and frequency of the waves that created it. The higher the waves, the stronger the rip current.

Rip currents pull water away from the shoreline and out to sea rapidly. It is easy for people and animals to get caught in them. In fact, more than 80 percent of the rescues that lifeguards make in the ocean involve saving people caught in rip currents.

Sometimes it's easy to identify rip currents. Often, the water in a rip current looks muddy or sandy due to the large amount of sediment, or matter, caught in the current. As the rip current moves, it lifts the sediment off the ocean floor and pulls it out to sea.

Rip currents are sometimes called riptides or undertows. However, both of these names are incorrect. Rip currents don't tow things under the water and they have nothing to do with the tides.

Water that gathers at the shore can cause a rip current. The higher the waves, the stronger the rip current.

Backwash

Backwash is similar to a rip current. It is usually caused by high tides on steeply sloping beaches that rise sharply away from the water's edge. People often underestimate backwash because it often occurs in shallow water. However, the force is still strong enough to knock people right off of their feet. It can also pull a swimmer out into deeper water.

To avoid being knocked over by backwash, never put your back to oncoming waves. This way, you will see the waves coming and know when and how to react to them before they crash. If you are pulled into deeper water, let the current carry you until you are freed from it. Then, swim away from the current and toward the shoreline.

Shorebreak

Shorebreak usually happens when the tide is high. A large wave crashing directly onto a beach with little or no water under it is called shorebreak. This type of current can be very dangerous to swimmers.

If you get caught in these kinds of waves, you could be thrown hard against the beach. You could be **stunned** or hurt badly. Shorebreak is particularly dangerous to swimmers when the shore is lined with rocks instead of sand. If the waves at the beach look like shorebreak, it's best to wait for safer conditions and go swimming later.

Always heed the warning signs posted at the beach.

WARNING

DANGEROUS CONDITIONS INCLUDE:

STRONG CURRENT

DANGEROUS SHOREBREAK

HIGH SURF

SWIM AT YOUR OWN RISK

OCEAN CONDITIONS MAY CAUSE SERIOUS BODILY INJURY, PARALYSIS OR DEATH

DEPARTMENT OF PARKS AND RECREATION COUNTY OF MAUI

Deep water currents are formed in colder regions of the ocean. Here, the water becomes colder and saltier. This combination makes the water denser, causing it to sink to the bottom. The water continues to sink until it reaches a point where the surrounding water is the same density. Then it spreads out. This causes layers of density in the ocean.

The Gulf Stream is a large current of warm water that moves north and east from the tip of Florida to the coast of Ireland. This current carries warm water into the North Atlantic Ocean. The water then cools and sinks in the Norwegian Sea.

Gravity and density are the natural forces that make ocean waters move. Deep water's density can change when its temperature or salinity (the amount of salt contained in the water) changes. Dense material sinks below less dense material because it is heavier. When surface water gets colder and saltier, and therefore denser, it sinks deep into the ocean.

Deep water in the North Atlantic follows currents and eventually makes its way toward the equator, where it warms up again. It eventually returns to the North Atlantic and repeats this cycle.

Deep water currents can be powerful forces. These currents help move huge icebergs from place to place. About 80 to 90 percent of an iceberg's mass is submerged. Some reach well below the ocean's surface. That means that the part you see above the water is only a tiny fraction of the iceberg's size!

Scientists call the water that sits between the deep and surface ocean water the thermocline. Water below the thermocline is dark and too far from light for photosynthesis to occur. Because of this, the creatures that live in deep water depend on currents to carry food and nutrients to them from other parts of the ocean.

Deep water currents

The ocean is very large and very powerful. If one doesn't follow basic safety guidelines in and around the ocean, accidents can occur. This chapter **emphasizes** precautions you can take at the beach that will help keep you safe. Some of these precautions include learning how to swim, swimming with other people, and learning to recognize dangerous situations before going into the water. Following these safety tips can make a swim in the ocean an enjoyable experience for everyone. Let's look at some ways to stay safe in the ocean.

When swimming in the ocean, always swim with a friend. Never go into the water without looking for dangerous situations first.

Learn to Swim

Not everyone knows how to swim. Learning to swim is the best thing you can do to keep safe in the ocean. It is a common misconception that the ocean is naturally safe to play in. As we learned in the previous chapter, there are hidden dangers in the waters of the sea. If you don't know what you're doing in the water, then the ocean can be a deadly trap.

Thankfully, there are many resources available for helping people learn how to swim. Learning to swim should be viewed as fun and necessary if you are going to be at the beach. At the very least, you should be able to **tread** water if you are planning to spend time at the beach. That way, you can keep your head above water. Once you have learned to tread water, you've started learning to respect and enjoy swimming.

Never Swim Alone

Always swim with a lifeguard present. Lifeguards can see dangers in the water that you might not be able to see for yourself. Lifeguards are trained professionals who can help in an emergency. They are at beaches and other swimming areas to make sure everyone has a safe, enjoyable time swimming.

It is also a good idea to swim with a friend. The lifeguard has a lot of people to look after on the beach. Swimming with a friend ensures that you will have someone looking out for you.

Warning flags are often used to alert swimmers to the conditions of the water. Make sure to observe the warning flags and swim with caution. And always swim within designated swimming areas.

THE FOLLOWING ARE PROHIBITED:
Alcoholic Beverages   Animals
Ball Playing   Camping
Flying Disc   Littering

Violators are subject to a fine, imprisonment or both
Auth.: ROH, as amended

Department of Parks and Recreation
City & County of Honolulu

LIFEGUARD
ON DUTY

Know Your Swimming Location

When choosing your swimming spot, make sure to steer clear of dangerous areas. Don't swim near piers or other large structures in the water. Don't swim near diving areas or other places where people might be entering the water quickly.

Never dive into water that you are unfamiliar with. You never know if sand beneath the surface of the water has shifted in the current since the last time you were there. If you have never been swimming there before, it may be hard to see the bottom. That means you may not know how close coral or rocks are to the surface of the water.

It is also a good idea to avoid aquatic plants and wildlife if you see them in the water. It's easy to get tangled up in seaweed or other plant life.

Lifeguards keep an eye out for people in trouble in the water.

General Ocean Safety

In some places it is **customary** to wait an hour after you eat before swimming. This is just a myth. However, there are some things you should be aware of before you enter the water. There are some warning signs your body gives you to let you know that you should not go swimming.

Never swim if you are feeling tired or cold, or if you have been in the sun for an extended period of time. You may be dehydrated and not realize it. If you are cold or tired and get caught up in a difficult current, you may be unable to swim to save yourself.

Swimming Safely in Strong Currents

Despite observing proper safety precautions and planning ahead, even the most prepared swimmers can get caught in dangerous currents. If you find yourself being pulled by a current you may make a **frantic** attempt to swim against it.

Unfortunately, swimming against the current will do little more than tire you out. Even the best swimmers may find it impossible to swim against powerful rip currents. If you are caught in a rip current that is pulling you away from shore, the safest thing to do is swim parallel to the shore, swimming sideways out of the rip current. Once you are out of the current, you can more easily swim back to shore. A similar rule applies to lateral currents. If you are caught in a lateral current, swim across it and toward the shore to free yourself from it.

Some Swimming Activities
Requiring Caution

Wind Surfing

Snorkeling

Scuba Diving

Water Skiing

The Powerful Ocean

We have seen that swimming in the ocean can be a dangerous affair. But it can also be fun and a safe activity. As long as you follow proper safety rules, there is little to worry about.

The currents of our oceans can be dangerous forces, but they are also important to our planet. They affect the weather in different parts of the world. They also provide food for some ocean creatures by carrying it from far away places.

The oceans' waters move all around Earth. If you are ever at the beach, look at the waves as they crash on the shore. Try to imagine where that water has been before it reached you!

It's important to have respect for the ocean and its currents. It is also very important to understand how and why currents work. If you find yourself caught in a current, it's important to remember not to try to swim against it. Let it carry you out until it weakens, and you can swim out of it. If it starts to take you out too far, swim across it. Remembering simple rules such as these can help save your life in an ocean emergency.

Glossary

customary *adj.* according to custom; usual.

emphasizes *v.* stresses; calls attention to.

frantic *adj.* very much excited; wild with rage, fear, pain, or grief.

stunned *adj.* dazed; bewildered; shocked; overwhelmed.

tread *v.* to keep the body straight in the water with the head above the surface by moving the arms and legs.